Superstars of NASCAR

by Todd Kortemeier

AMICUS HIGH INTEREST • AMICUS INK

Amicus High Interest and Amicus Ink
are imprints of Amicus
P.O. Box 1329, Mankato, MN 56002
www.amicuspublishing.us

Library of Congress Cataloging-in-Publication Data
Title: Superstars of NASCAR / by Todd Kortemeier.
Other titles: Superstars of the National Association for Stock Car Auto
Racing
Description: Mankato, MN : Amicus High Interest, [2016] | Series: Pro
Sports Superstars |
Includes index.
Identifiers: LCCN 2015034274 (print) | LCCN 2015050426 (ebook) |
   ISBN 9781607539407 (hardcover)
   ISBN 9781681510309 (pdf ebook)
   ISBN 9781681521053 (paperback)
Subjects: LCSH: Stock car drivers--Biography--Juvenile literature. |
NASCAR (Association)--History--Juvenile literature.
Classification: LCC GV1029.9.S74 K67 2016 (print) | LCC GV1029.9.S74
(ebook) | DDC 796.720922--dc23
LC record available at http://lccn.loc.gov/2015034274

Photo Credits: Todd Warshaw/Getty Images for NASCAR/Getty Images,
cover; Nigel Kinrade/NKP/AP Images, 2, 20; Nam Y. Huh/AP Images, 4–5,
22; Bettmann/Corbis, 6; Michael Conroy/AP Images, 8–9; Donald Miralle/
Allsport/Getty Images, 10–11; Carlos Osorio/AP Images, 12; Walter G Arce/
Cal Sport Media/AP Images, 15; Jared C. Tilton/Getty Images, 16–17; Kyle
Ocker/Icon Sportswire, 18

Produced for Amicus by The Peterson Publishing Company
and Red Line Editorial.

Editor Arnold Ringstad
Designer Becky Daum

Printed in the United States of America
North Mankato, MN

HC 10 9 8 7 6 5 4 3 2 1
PB 10 9 8 7 6 5 4 3 2 1

TABLE OF CONTENTS

HIGH-SPEED ACTION

All sports have exciting moments. But NASCAR has the fastest action. **Stock cars** are powerful machines. They zoom around the **track** at high speeds. Each one needs a skilled driver. These are some of the best.

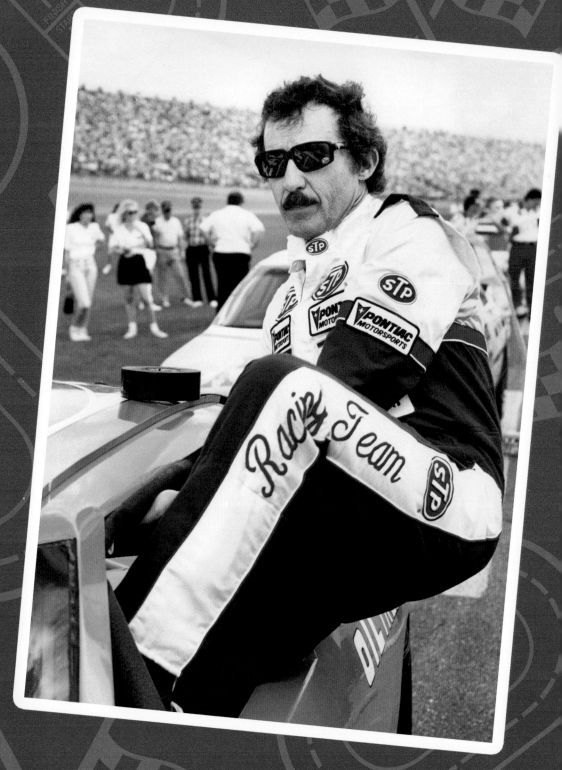

RICHARD PETTY

Richard Petty's nickname was "The King." He won 200 races. No driver has won more. Petty retired in 1992. He later owned his own race team. He was voted into the NASCAR **Hall of Fame** in 2010.

JEFF GORDON

Jeff Gordon was named **Rookie** of the Year in 1991. In 1995 he won his first **title**. In 1997 he won the Daytona 500.

Richard Petty's last race was Jeff Gordon's first.

DALE EARNHARDT

Dale Earnhardt won 76 races. But he struggled to win the Daytona 500. It took him 24 years. He finally won the race in 1998. Earnhardt died after a racing crash in 2001. Afterward NASCAR made many safety improvements.

DALE EARNHARDT JR.

Dale Earnhardt Jr. is the son of a legend. His first race was in 1999. He won 25 races by 2015. He is a fan favorite.

Earnhardt's grandfather Ralph also raced. He won a NASCAR title in 1956.

TONY STEWART

Tony Stewart can race all kinds of cars. He won an **IndyCar** title in 1997. He then decided to try NASCAR. He won a title in 2002. Since 2010 he has been sponsored by motor oil company Mobil 1.

Stewart twice drove IndyCar and NASCAR races in the same day.

JIMMIE JOHNSON

Jimmie Johnson joined NASCAR in 2002. He soon became a champion. He won five titles in a row from 2006 to 2010. He added another in 2013. Johnson drives the number 48 car.

BRAD KESELOWSKI

Brad Keselowski grew up in a racing family. He won a title in 2012. He fell just short of another one in 2014. He won 17 races by 2015.

KEVIN HARVICK

Kevin Harvick won the Daytona 500 in 2007. In 2014 he took the next step. He won five races and his first title.

NASCAR has had many great superstars. Who will be next?

Harvick's nickname is "Happy."

NASCAR FAST FACTS

Founded: 1947

Number of Races per Season: 36

Drivers per Race: 43

Drivers per Season: 51 drivers in the 2015 Sprint Cup Series

Most Wins: 200, Richard Petty

Most Championships: 7, Dale Earnhardt and Richard Petty

Fastest Driver: Bill Elliott, 212.809 mph, 1987

WORDS TO KNOW

Hall of Fame – a group of drivers that NASCAR leaders consider the best ever

IndyCar – a type of racing where the cars' wheels are open to the air, rather than being under the car's body

rookie – a first-year driver

stock car – the kind of car that competes in NASCAR, designed to look like everyday road cars, but with powerful engines, special tires, and other racing features

title – a NASCAR championship victory; drivers who win races throughout the season earn a chance to compete for the overall championship

track – the closed roads on which NASCAR races are held; they are usually shaped like ovals and have seats around the edges for fans

LEARN MORE

Books

Challen, Paul. *NASCAR Racing*. New York: PowerKids Press, 2015.

Kopp, Megan. *NASCAR*. New York: AV2 by Weigl, 2014.

Roberts, Angela. *NASCAR's Greatest Drivers*. New York: Random House, 2009.

Websites

Fox Sports: NASCAR
http://www.foxsports.com/nascar
Read the latest news about NASCAR.

NASCAR.com
http://www.nascar.com
Learn more about drivers at the official NASCAR website.

INDEX